The BIBLE

and the

ENVIRONMENT

by Meg Guillebaud

THE BIBLE AND THE ENVIRONMENT

THE BIBLE AND THE ENVIRONMENT
INTRODUCTION

My brother is a keen environmentalist. For years I have listened to him talking about the damage we human beings are doing to the environment. Like many other Christians, I paid lip service to the fact that we ought to care for God's creation but it was only in the last year or so I began to take seriously what the Bible really says about creation and how we as human beings, particularly Christians, ought to relate to it.

I remember a talk given by the Bishop of Cyangugu, Rwanda, about 4 years ago, when he talked about all creation praising God. Yes, it was there in the Bible, but I didn't really take in what was being said. For years I have taught from Romans 1:20, asking my students what creation can teach us about God, but had never taken seriously the idea that if God made such a wonderful world which speaks so eloquently about him, then it follows that he cares for it and wants his people to care for it as well.

Some years ago I had read the Five Marks of Mission[1] defined by the worldwide Anglican Communion, adopted at the Lambeth Conference in 1988:

1   To proclaim the good news of the Kingdom
2   To teach, baptise and nurture new believers
3   To respond to human need by loving service
4   To seek to transform unjust structures of society
5   To strive to safeguard the integrity of creation and sustain and renew the life of the earth.

Like many other evangelical Christians, I had considered the first three marks all that I needed to concern myself with. When I wrote my book *Rwanda - The Land God Forgot?*[2] I had been challenged by the need for Christians to fight injustice, but the last mark of mission was still way out of my thinking.

Then, two years ago several things all happened at once. I met someone who was involved in the work of A Rocha, a Christian environmental organisation which had begun its work in Portugal. I had heard that Crosslinks supported them before I had come to Rwanda 15 years ago and had been mildly intrigued by the idea that a Christian Mission could support an environmental organisation. But soon after that I was caught up in the aftermath of the tragedy of genocide in Rwanda, and my thoughts and energies went into other things

Now I learned about the work that had been done, putting Christian principles into action, and how whole areas worldwide had been transformed. I read Dave Bookless' book, *Planetwise*[3], and was challenged to be more active in my approach to the environment. What really helped me was to see how Biblical his approach was. What I saw in the Bible finally convinced me that this was no peripheral issue but should be central to all Christians.

At about this time I also saw Al Gore's DVD, *An Inconvenient Truth*, showing what an environmental disaster mankind has made of our world and was frightened by the extent of the damage done to the environment since the Industrial Revolution. I am aware that some of what he said is controversial and that some people regard him as a political propagandist, but it still constituted a wake-up call for me.

Then, thirdly, in 2008, at a conference for mission partners organised by my Mission, CMS, I was confronted by the need for Christians to be actively involved in environmental issues.

Jordan Pickering, in his article *Evangelicalism and Ecology*[4], states that there are four major ecological crises faced today:
- Massive reductions in bio-diversity caused by deforestation, poisons and bad farming methods.
- Climatic change caused by pollutants, including carbon dioxide and methane, (a by-product of industrial beef and rice farming).

- Pollution by industrial, chemical and post-consumer wastes.
- Soil erosion and desertification caused by deforestation and poor farming methods.

The Government of Rwanda has been active in several environmental issues, limiting the cutting of trees and the digging of new gravel pits as well as forbidding the use of plastic bags, which so litter the countryside of many other African countries. However, just as I had had to be convinced of the importance of this issue from the Scriptures, I felt it important to write this book, so that Christians, in Rwanda particularly, should be convinced that this is something that all should be involved in. Only as I started to write did I feel that perhaps I should also write it in English so that it could be used elsewhere.

There are so many people I should thank for getting me interested in this project: My brother, Professor John Guillebaud (John, I am sorry it has taken so long to convert me); the authors of several books which have helped (see Bibliography); and the inspiration from the work of A Rocha. I particularly want to thank Caroline and Henry Pomeroy from Send a Cow, Rwanda, whose enthusiasm has kept me going; the group, Christian Action for the Environment in Rwanda (CEAR) in Kigali, for their constructive criticisms and suggestions; and several of my missionary colleagues with whom I have had much lively correspondence especially Dr Keith Fernando and Dr Paula Sage; also my cousins Frank and Susan Grenfell for their helpful input. Any resulting conclusions and opinions are mine, as well as any mistakes. A very special thank you to Sophia Jenkins for the lovely illustrations and to Caroline Pomeroy for the cover photo taken on a lovely day in the Rugezi Wetlands.

Mark 16:9-20 is often ignored since it is not found in the earliest manuscripts of the Gospel. (In my Bible it appears in italics and as a footnote.) Yet the Holy Spirit allowed it to be retained down the ages. In Mark's version of the Great Commission, Jesus tells his disciples "Go into all the world and preach the gospel **to all creation**." (My emphasis.) However difficult it might be to envision preaching to non-human beings, the gospel is not just about saving souls, or even meeting the needs of the whole person, it is - or should be- good news for all creation.

Dave Bookless writes 'Just as all Christians are called to pray, meet together, study God's word and share the good news, so caring for creation is essential to following Jesus Christ.'[5] Following Jesus means that we must look at his world through God's eyes: to see that he made it beautiful and gave us the responsibility to care for it; to see that God cares for all that he has made, not just us human beings; to understand that the Bible is the story of God and the whole of his creation.

I have divided the book into 5 parts with an introduction to each, looking at relevant issues. Then I have given a few Bible Studies on that issue (sometimes just one, sometimes as many as three.) At the end of each introduction and study are discussion questions for consideration, alone or in group study. I hope that as we study God's word together we shall see that we have got our relationship with the earth all wrong and will seek to put that right as disciples of Jesus Christ.

Notes

1   www.cofe.anglican.org/faith/mission/missionevangelism.html.
2   Guillebaud, 2001, pp 323-330.
3   Bookless, 2008, *Planetwise*.
4   Pickering Jordan, n.d. article, "Christians and Ecology"
     www.studenty.org.za/resources/.
5   Bookless, 2008, p.16.

PART I   **ALL OF GOD'S CREATURES**

Years ago in Rwanda when there was no Akagera Game Park, lions and leopards roamed where they would, frequently killing human beings and being killed in their turn. Then, in 1934, the Colonial Government made a Game Reserve near the Akagera River and said that within that area no wild animals were to be killed. This was partly as a tourist attraction but also so that wildlife would have somewhere where they were safe and to encourage the lions and leopards to stay where they would not be harmed. To reinforce this, the Government put a 'buffer zone' between the Game Park and where people lived. No one was allowed to settle in this area but it was where hunters, with the necessary licence, could kill game for eating. Soon lions learned that if they roamed too far from the Akagera they would be killed and so they were content to eat the deer as they had for centuries past.

However, from 1990 during the war and the break-down of law and order leading to the genocide, and in the years following, when there was so much to do in restoring the country, the old laws relating to the Game Park were ignored. Incoming poachers from Tanzania killed many of the animals as a cheap source of 'bush meat' which could be sold at a huge profit. Then returning refugees, with their cattle, settled in the old hunting reserves. Unfortunately the lions did not understand the difference between cattle and the deer they were accustomed to kill. They killed cattle and, sometimes, people, and were in their turn killed, until very few were left.

Now the policy is for the Game Park to pay compensation to local farmers for damage caused by lions or elephants. As a result they are no longer being killed and their population is once again slowly rising adding to the tourist attraction.

5

In the Nyungwe Forest, in the south of Rwanda, the last elephant was killed by poachers in 1990. You can see its skull in the Uwinka Tourist Centre. As a result, the clearing of the undergrowth which elephants used to do no longer happens. Smaller animals can now no longer travel freely through the forest, and some trees and flowers are being choked to death.

There is tension between those living around the Virunga National Park and those caring for the environment where the last remaining mountain gorillas live. The former want more land to cultivate whereas the forest is needed to provide safety and food for the gorillas.

Would it matter if these gorillas or lions in the Akagera like the elephant in the Nyungwe died out? Should the Virunga be preserved for the gorillas? How can the needs of the people nearby be met? Why is the Rwanda Government so concerned to preserve the National Parks? Is it only a matter for Government or should we all be concerned? Why?

As I have asked these questions in recent months I have received various responses:
Yes - these animals attract tourists who bring needed money into the country.
No - lions kill humans and their stock. Gorillas are keeping needed farmland from the people in the area.
Yes - lions kept down the deer which are now over-grazing the Game Park and the grass is now becoming poorer, threatening all the animals. Elephants cleared the undergrowth and provided pathways for smaller animals as well as humans.
Yes - all these animals were created by God and give him pleasure.
No - God gave mankind dominion over animals, so it is up to us to decide how we control them.
Yes - we have a God-given responsibility to steward God's earth and its resources.

Perhaps you have other answers. Yet important though lions, elephants and gorillas may be, many more, smaller creatures are disappearing through the thoughtless destruction of their habitats. Tearing up the hedgerows in Britain so that there could be more intensive farming, for instance, has led to the decline of many songbirds, just as the destruction of wetlands in Rwanda and Uganda has led to a disastrous decline in the beautiful crowned cranes (golden crested cranes). Chopping down virgin forest or draining wetlands may provide more land for cultivation for increasing population but in the process contributes to climate change and the destruction of bio-diversity in the destroyed habitats.

Unless we realise how much God loves all that he has made and appreciate the intrinsic value of every creature and plant, these habitats will continue to be destroyed for the benefit of just one species - mankind. Let us see what the Bible teaches about creation.

Bible Study 1.1   <u>**God and his creation**</u>
<u>Starter Question</u>
Do all animals, plants and trees have an intrinsic worth? Should they all
be preserved? What about mosquitoes? Or killing for food?

1   Who was involved in creation?
Genesis 1:1

John 1:1-3

Colossians 1:15-17

2   What do we learn about creation from the following verses?
Genesis 1:31 (see also **1 Timothy 4:4**)

Job 34:14-15

Psalm 24:1

Psalm 74:16-17

Isaiah 45:18

Hebrews 11:3

3   What is the purpose of creation?
Job 12:7-9

Psalm 19:1-4a

Romans 1:20

Putting together what we can find out from these verses:
- We see that unlike all other creation stories in the surrounding nations, the God of Israel created the heavens and the earth out of nothing.
- Surrounding nations worshipped the sun, moon and stars as gods. Genesis 1 and Psalm 74 tells us that God created the sun, moon and stars!
- The triune God was involved in creation.
- All creation, not just human beings, was created by the Lord Jesus Christ and for him.
- Yet the earth was created to be inhabited by man
- Everything that God made was good.
- Everything that God made proclaims his glory
- We can learn about God through studying his creation.

You may have found other points to add to these but it is important to recognise the above points before we go on to further study.

Psalm 19 is a fascinating study. The first few verses tell how creation shows God's glory but verses 7-10 speak of God's word. As Bookless (2008) points out, God speaks to us in two ways: through his works (of creation), and through his word (the Bible). If we only had his works we would have an incomplete picture of who God is, but if we only study his word, again our picture of God is incomplete. We need both for a full understanding of who God is. (p.27)

Discussion Questions
1 What signs of God's 'invisible qualities' (**Romans 1:20**) do you see in creation? What can we learn about him from the beasts, birds and plants (**Job 12:7-9**)?
2 Why do you think that so many Psalms speak of God in relation to creation?
3 How does creation help us to worship God?

Bible Study 1.2   <u>**Creation and Man**</u>

<u>Starter Question</u>

How can we reconcile the needs of people living near a game reserve with the needs of the animals?

1   What can we find about human being's relationship to creation in the following verses?

Genesis 1:27

Genesis 1:28

Genesis 2:5

Genesis 2:7

Genesis 2:8-9

2   What do we learn about the value God place's on mankind in these verses? Do they imply that He does not also care for the rest of creation?

Psalm 8:3-4

Psalm 8:5-8

Matthew 6:26

Matthew 6:28-30

Matthew 10:28-30

3   What does the following passage tell us about God's relationship to humanity?

Acts 17:24-28

Note:
- People were made in God's image, male and female both in his image.
- God gave each group of people their own times and areas in which to live.
- People were also made of the dust of the earth like all other animals.
- They were given authority over all other created things.
- But they were also put into the garden God had given them to care for it and to till it, and eventually move out giving the same care wherever they went. In fact, without man to work it there was no garden!
- Humans may seem insignificant compared with some other created things in our universe but God has chosen to rule through them.
- Humans were created to have fellowship with God, and to relate, not only to our neighbours but also to the whole created world.

From an early age children think that everything revolves around them. But as they grow older they realise that they need to relate to others and to share with them. In a similar way, because as Christians we believe that we human beings are the pinnacle of God's creation, we often selfishly consider that everything else is there for us and can be used in any way we please. The Bible does not allow this view. The whole earth and everything in it belongs to God (**Psalm 24:1**). Yet he has given authority to humans over other created things. **Psalm 8:5-6** makes it clear that we are ruling them as his regents. The fact that they are under our feet (**Psalm 8:6**) does not mean that they are to be trampled on but that they are subjects to be cared for and ruled with God's justice and compassion. Throughout the Old Testament, God wanted the kings he had set in authority to rule as servants.

Two words are used in the creation accounts to describe how humans are to treat other created things: *radah* and *abad*:
i   The Hebrew word used in **Genesis 1:26, 28** *radah* or dominion is in fact a strong word usually implying gaining authority by conquest.

11

But it is God's gift to us and a good ruler uses his authority even over the conquered people with compassion and justice if he wants peace in the defeated land.

4   The word *radah* is used in the following verses. What is being said?
Job 25:2

Psalm 22:27-28

1 Kings 4:24-25

5   How were the kings of Israel meant to behave towards their subjects?
Deuteronomy 17:14-20

2 Samuel 5:2

ii   The Hebrew word *abad* used in **Genesis 2:15** means to care for or do service to. It is used about 150 times in the Old Testament, usually in connection with religious service to God.

6   The word *abad* is used in the following verses. What is being said?
Genesis 3:23

Proverbs 12:11

Ezekiel 36:33-35

Putting these two words together we see that human authority over the rest of creation is intended to be used as God's authority is used; not trampling over it and despoiling it, but loving it and caring for it, so that it produces more not less.

There is another Hebrew word we must remember. The name, Adam, for the first man, is taken from *adamah* which means earth. Adam was a very earthy man, taken from the very fabric of the earth.

Just as we need to hold in balance the concepts of *radah* and *abad,* so we need also to hold in balance the two aspects of our nature: we are both created beings like other animals and we are made in the image of God.

If we forget the second and think that we are merely animals like others, it might be tempting to say, as some do in the West, that the world would recover quicker if all humans were destroyed. But if we forget that we were created from the dust of the earth, like all animals, we may feel that we have a right to treat them as we wish. Both aspects of our creation need to be remembered and held in balance.

Discussion Questions
1 How can the way we treat the environment be seen as worshipping God?
2 How is authority meant to be exercised with regard to creation? What does this mean in practice?
3 Are there things we should change in the way that we treat other created things? Can we make a commitment to change and be held accountable by others in the group?

Bible Study 1.3 <u>The fall of man and its effect on the whole created order</u>

<u>Starter Question</u>
We have seen that the world that God created in love was good, but as we look around us we see many evidences of damage to that world. Why? What has caused it?

Whatever we blame for this damage – the industrial revolution and the careless exploitation of the earth's resources or human ignorance and greed – the Bible tells us plainly that the root cause is sin.

God intended mankind to live in harmony with himself, with each other and with his world. **Genesis 3** tells how that harmony was destroyed. Read the whole chapter and note the consequences of mankind's disobedience to God.

1   How were relationships with God changed?
Genesis 3:8

Genesis 3:16

Genesis 3:23-24

Note:
*   Adam and Eve hid from God.
*   Eve's relationship to God was changed. Instead of looking to Him for fulfilment, her desire was primarily for her husband .
*   Ultimately they were expelled from the garden where they had enjoyed such intimacy with God. **Isaiah 59:2** tells us that sin always separates us from God.

2   How were relationships to each other changed?
Genesis 3:7

Genesis 3:12-13

Genesis 3:16

Note:
- The openness they had previously enjoyed together was now covered up.
- They blamed each other .
- Their relationship of equality and complementarity was exchanged for one of domination. It is only in Christ that equality is restored (**Galatians 3:28**).

3   How were relationships to created things changed?
Genesis 3:17-19

Genesis 3:21

Note:
- Work became labour rather than the joy it had been .
- Animals were killed to give them covering.

4   What do these verses tell us of other results of man's disobedience to God?
Leviticus 26:39-43

Romans 5:12

Romans 8:19-25

1 John 5:19

Note:
- All creation suffered as a result of sin of mankind.
- Since God had given us stewardship of his creation and we had chosen to obey Satan rather than God, Satan assumed authority as ruler of this world (see also **Luke 4:3-7; John 12:31; 2 Corinthians 4:4**).
- The land suffered not only for our sins, but the sins of our fathers. It was as the Israelites confessed their own sins as well as those of their ancestors that God remembered their land.

5   What do these verses tell us about the relationship between man's sin and the land?

Genesis 4:10-12

2 Chronicles 7:14

Ezra 9:11

Jeremiah 2:7

Jeremiah 12:4

Hosea 4:1-3

Isaiah 24:4-5

Note:
- The land was polluted by sin, indeed it was cursed and it involved hard labour for it to bring forth fruit. It needed cleansing and healing. This does not mean that we can cleanse it by clearing the land but that there is a spiritual dimension involved and only God can remove the curse as his people seek his forgiveness.

- These verses speak of the relationship between sin and mankind, yet it is not as a direct consequence. It is the sin of all mankind that has led to a damaged environment, not necessarily of the people living in a particular area. In the same way, anyone may suffer from sickness or disease because we live in a sinful world but this is not necessarily a direct consequence of their own actions.
- Yet **Romans 8:19-25** also speaks of hope. As soon as sin entered the world, God immediately set his plans in motion to restore these damaged relationships. This will be the subject of our next few studies, but there is one more question to ask.

6 When was the plan for redemption formed and what would be affected by it?

Ephesians 1:3-4

Ephesians 1:9-10

John 16:11

Discussion Questions
1 What signs do we see in the world around us of the breakdown of our relationships:
- to God?
- to other people?
- to the created order?
2 What is the effect of people's sin on the earth? How is this manifested (**Isaiah 24:4-5**)?
3 Have you any hope for this world? Why, or why not?

PART 2 GOD AND THE WORLD

Not all Christian traditions have seen Creation as a resource to be used at will by mankind. It can be argued that we are the poorer for having abandoned some of those traditions.

Perhaps the best known is St Francis of Assisi who had a special love of all created beings. He tried to "persuade the emperor to make a special law that men should then provide well for the birds and the beasts, as well as for the poor, so that all might have occasion to rejoice in the Lord." Most of our pictures of St Francis show him surrounded by birds and beasts listening to his sermons. "Francis's love of nature also stands out in bold relief in the world he moved in. He delighted to commune with the wild flowers, the crystal spring, and the friendly fire, and to greet the sun as it rose upon the fair Umbrian vale." His best known hymn is the "Canticle of the Sun" in which all of creation brings praise to God[1].

Another example of care for creation comes from Celtic Christianity which developed in the British Isles and Northern France in the 5th - 6th centuries. In contrast to the forms of Christianity known elsewhere in Europe, "the Celtic church leaders were openly critical of worldly wealth and status"[2], travelling on foot and using only basic necessities for life. They spent hours in prayer and Bible study in their monasteries but also had a "conviction that knowledge of God could be deepened through secular scholarship as well as sacred study. The former informed the latter (indeed, there was little distinction made between the two). Intellectual ability was seen as a Christian virtue to be prized; knowledge of all kinds valued. All of this served to enrich understanding of the divine revelation."[3]

The cross was at the heart of their faith and the great high crosses of the Celtic lands still bear witness to this. They were very aware of the glory of the natural world which proclaimed the power of the Creator and inspired awe and wonder, but they recognised that it was fallen and in need of redemption[4]. Their best known hymn is "St Patrick's Breastplate"[5] which is strongly Trinitarian but also invokes the powers of nature as protection. The Celtic Christians saw the natural world as enhancing their knowledge of God. "The God who made the world is the same God who will protect Christians from all dangers."[6]

At the Synod of Whitby in 664AD, in the interests of unity, the decision was taken to unite the British Church behind the Roman Church brought by St Augustine of Canterbury with its much more hierarchical form of Christianity and emphasis on Church buildings, wealth and status. Sadly, many of the specifically Celtic emphases, such as the importance of creation and the equality of the sexes, were lost and have only been rediscovered towards the end of the 20th century. However, some Christians fear this rediscovery of Celtic worship, saying that it was originally based on Druidic or pagan belief. It is, indeed, possible that the Celts fell into the trap of worshipping trees and rivers (or their spirits) as well as the Creator, which led to many of their prayers being banned during the Reformation.

Alistair Petrie warns about this syncretism in Celtic Christianity. In effect, he says, they identified the Creator with his Creation[7]. He says: "We must at all times worship the Creator and be faithful stewards of His creation, while at the same time avoiding the subtle danger of making creation the object of our worship (see Romans 1:25). As Christians we are called not *out* of the world, but rather *into* it, in order to make a difference as salt and light *to* the world. Part of our concern, then, necessitates dealing with the issues of acid rain, the ozone layer and the pollution of our environment growing at an alarming rate, as well as the ensuing issues of war, famine and disease"[8] (his emphases).

The following story from the Celtic tradition shows their sense of God being worshipped in all Creation: "It was often the habit of the man of God [St Benno] to go about the fields in meditation and prayer: and once as he passed by a certain marsh, a talkative frog was croaking in its slimy waters: and lest it should disturb his contemplation, he bade it to be a Seraphian, inasmuch as all frogs in Seraphus are mute. But when he had gone on a little way, he called to mind the saying in Daniel [the Canticle called the Benedicite]: '*O ye whales and all that move in the waters, bless ye the Lord. O all ye beasts and cattle, bless ye the Lord.*' And fearing lest the singing of the frogs might perchance be more agreeable to God than his own praying, he again issued his command to them, that they should praise God in their accustomed fashion: and soon the air and fields were vehement with their conversation."[9]

Richard Bauckham, commenting on this story says that St Benno was wrong to think that frogs only praise God in their croaking[10]. So do they in the way they leap and swim and in the colours of their skin!

BIBLE STUDY 2.1   ALL CREATION PRAISES GOD

Starter Question

In what ways could we make creation, rather than God, the object of our worship?

1   What do the following verses teach us about worship? What is giving glory to God and how?

Psalm 69:34

Psalm 96:11-12

Psalm 98:7-8

Psalm 150:6

Luke 19:40

Philippians 2:10-11

Revelation 5:13

The *Benedicite*, which challenged St Benno, is a canticle which appears in the Apocropha and is an addition to the Daniel story. It is the song that Shadrach, Meshach and Abednego are said to have sung in the midst of the furnace as they walked with the Son of God. Because it was rejected by the Reformers, most Protestants would deny that it is part of Scripture, although it appears in the Anglican Prayer Book (see Article 6 which says that the books of the Apocropha are to be read "for example of life and instruction of manners" but not for doctrine)[11]. It was written in Greek, probably in the 2nd Century BC, and seems to be based on **Psalm 148**.

2   What is praising the Lord in **Psalm 148**? How many different things can you find?

Another passage which bears reading prayerfully is **Job 38-42**, where God's delight in his creation and demonstration of his power and wisdom, brings Job to repentance, as he humbly confesses his ignorance. Many scientists declare their wonder and awe at the glory of God increases as they find out more about creation. (See also **Psalm 66:1-2; Psalm 97:1-6; Psalm 103:22; Psalm 104:10-23; Isaiah 40:12; 42:10**)

3   What do the following verses tell us about God's relationship with creation?
Psalm 50:10-11

Psalm 104:24-25

Psalm 104:27-30

Psalm 104:31

Isaiah 43:20

The four living creatures of **Revelation 4:7** seem to represent all living beings, the lion as a wild beast, the eagle as a bird, the ox as a domestic animal and man at one with the rest of creation.

4   Consider the way the four living creatures worship God.
Revelation 4:8

Revelation 5:11-14

Yet in **Revelation 6** the four living creatures are involved in the calling forth of judgement on the earth as the seven seals are opened.

5   What is the result of opening these seals?
The first seal **Revelation 6:1-2**
The second seal **Revelation 6:3-4**

The third seal **Revelation 6:5-6**

The fourth seal **Revelation 6:7-8**

Discussion Questions
1   How does the fact that all creation worships God and gives him glory, help us in our worship?
2   Does this affect the way we look at creation?
3   What does **Revelation 6** say to us about the state of the world today?
4   Donald Macleod says: "Theologically, the primary function of the creation is to serve as a revelation of God. To spoil the creation is to disable it from performing this function"[12] Do you agree or disagree with this statement? Why or why not?

BIBLE STUDY 2.2   GOD AND THE LAND

There are over 2,000 mentions of land in the Old Testament and over 250 in the New Testament.[10] This gives some indication of how important it is to God. The link that human beings have with the land is still strong in countries like Rwanda. However, in other parts of the world, as more and more people move into cities, their links with the land become fewer and their understanding of God through natural things become less.

Starter Question

Do you think that city dwellers have indeed lost their connection to the land? How does this affect their thinking? Could it explain why pollution has been allowed to get out of hand, with accompanying degradation of the environment?

1   What does God say about the land in the following verses?
Leviticus 25:1-7

Leviticus 25:23

Psalm 24:1

Psalm 66:4

Psalm 97:1

Proverbs 16:4

Jeremiah 29:4-7

Acts 17:26

From these verses we see:
- The earth is the Lord's.
- The earth, in some way, recognises that he is Lord and rejoices before him.
- Everything has been created for a purpose.
- God has given it to human beings to care for it.
- We are to seek the prosperity of the place where we have been set.
- The land itself needs a Sabbath rest, not only man.

2   From the following verses, what can we find out about the land's reaction to man's sin?
Leviticus 18:24-28

Deuteronomy 28:22-28

Isaiah 24:4-5

Jeremiah 12:4

Hosea 4:1-3

Romans 8:19-22

Compare the blessings and curses given in **Deuteronomy 28**. Although Israel as God's chosen people are referred to here, it gives an indication of the effect on the land of human sin.

3   What blessings are given as a result of obedience?
Deuteronomy 28:2-5

Deuteronomy 28:8

Deuteronomy 28:11-12

4   What curses result from disobedience?

Deuteronomy 28:22-24

Deuteronomy 28:38-40, 42

We also read that God brings judgement on the land because of mankind's sin.

5   What specific things are mentioned in these verses?

Amos 4:7

Ezekiel 14:13

Ezekiel 14:15

Ezekiel 14:17

Ezekiel 14:19-20

Malachi 4:6

Note:
- God's judgements are always to bring people to repent and so to heal their land (see **2 Chronicles 7:13-14**)

6   What does God say will happen when the final time for judgement comes?

Revelation 11:18

7   From the following verses what hope is there for the land?
2 Chronicles 7:12-14

Colossians 1:17

Colossians 1:20

Discussion Questions
1   How can we join with all creation in bringing glory to God?
2   Does the idea of the land itself rejoicing in God and mourning the sin of mankind have an effect on you?
3   What evidences do you see that God is bringing judgement on the land? How does this make you feel? What can we do about it?
4   Do you think that God will judge us for our mismanagement of the environment?

BIBLE STUDY 2.3   <u>JESUS AND THE LAND</u>

Starter Question

Consider the familiar Christmas Carol, based on the words of Psalm 98:

Joy to the World! The Lord is come;
Let earth receive her King;
Let every heart prepare him room;
And Heaven and nature sing.

Joy to the earth! The Saviour reigns;
Let men their songs employ;
While fields and floods, rocks, hills and plains
Repeat the sounding joy.

No more let sins and sorrows grow
Nor thorns infest the ground;
He comes to make his blessings flow
Far as the curse is found.

Why is it a matter of rejoicing for nature, including fields and rocks, that the Saviour has been born?

Probably the most familiar verse in the Bible is **John 3:16**. Yet we often fail to recognise exactly what is written. In the Kinyarwanda Bible the word 'world' is translated 'the people in the world' and indeed that is the way most of us would interpret it. The Greek word is *kosmos*, the word from which we get the English cosmology or study of the universe. 'The original meaning of this word, and one of the ways it continued to be used in Greek, was "order" or "decoration". It is a noun formed from the verb which means to arrange or set in order. It came to be the word used for the world because of early Greek belief that first there was chaos and then either one divinity or a combination of them brought order out of chaos - that is the *kosmos* - the ordering, arranging of everything. *Kosmos* is usually translated 'world'. It is much bigger than *ge* which refers to 'earth' alone.'[14] *Kosmos* is also used in NT to refer to the sum total of things that are opposed to Christ or to Life in the Spirit.[15]

It seems, then, that God loved the whole universe so much that he sent his Son into the world! Is this concept borne out elsewhere in the Bible?

1   Why and how were all things created?
John 1:1-3

Romans 11:36

Colossians 1:16

Colossians 1:17

Hebrews 1:2-3

Revelation 4:11

From these verses we see:
- The world was made by and through Christ.
- It was made for Christ and his glory.
- It is sustained by Christ.
- It was created by the will of God.

In the Temple which Solomon built, he created a place for the Ark of the Covenant which he called God's footstool, where God's presence was found. (**1 Chronicles 28:2**). In **Isaiah 66:1-2** and **Matthew 5:35** the earth is called 'God's footstool', what does this imply about the earth?

2   What do the following verses say about God's purposes in Christ Jesus for the redemption of the world?

Ephesians 1:7-10

Colossians 1:19-20

Romans 8:19-21

Matthew 28:18

Note:
- Just as all things were created through and for Christ so all things will be reconciled to God through his cross.
- God's plan is to unite all things in Christ.
- Creation itself will be set free from decay.
- The authority of Jesus covers the whole cosmos.

3   In **Matthew 24:37-38** Jesus compares the last days to the time of Noah so let us consider that familiar story found in **Genesis 6-9.**

Genesis 6:6-7   Why did God bring judgement on the earth?

Genesis 6:18   How many humans did God rescue?

Genesis 7:2-3   Why did God include all the animals on the ark?

Genesis 8:21-22   What did God promise after the ark landed?

Genesis 9:12-16   To whom is the rainbow a sign of God's saving covenant?

Discussion Questions
1   How is your understanding of the cross affected by realising that Jesus died to redeem 'all things'?

2   Noah has been described as 'the arch-conservationist'. What does his story add to your understanding of the world in God's purposes?
3   Does it make a difference to see the earth as God's footstool?
4   James Jones, Bishop of Liverpool wrote: "The earth is here for us to delight in, to manage, to serve but its centre is inhabited by Christ, not us. It is a blasphemy to usurp Christ's place"[16] What do you make of this statement? How might it change your approach to conservation of the earth?

Notes on Part 2

1   *The Catholic Encyclopedia,* "St Francis of Assisi", www.newadvent.org/cathen) .
2   McGrath, Alister, 1998, *Historical Theology,* p. 97.
3   Rhymer, David, "Where does Celtic Christianity lead us?" www.peran.org.uk.
4   Article, "Celtic Christian History", www.st_cuthberts.net/celhist.htm.
5   *Wikipedia,* "St Patrick's Breastplate", tr. Alexander, Cecil F. (1823-1895), http://en.wikisource.org.
6   McGrath, Alister, 1998, p.98.
7   Petrie, Alistair, 2000, *Releasing Heaven on Earth,* p. 103-104.
8   *Ibid.,* p. 28.
9   tr. Waddell, Helen, 1934, *Beasts and Saints,* in Bauckham, Richard, "Joining Creation's Praise of God", *Ecotheology 7.1,* 2002, p. 45-46.
10 *Ibid*
11 Bauckham, Richard, "Joining Creation's Praise of God", *Ecotheology 7.1,* 2002, p 46-47.
12 Statement of Rev Prof Donald Macleod, Free Church College, Edinburgh, in the Lingerbay Quarry Inquiry, an environmental inquiry on the Isle of Harris. www.alistairmcintosh.com/articles/1995_law&religion.htm.
13 Russ Parker, 2001, *Healing Wounded History,* p.8, as quoted by Bookless (2008), p.47.

14 Sage, Dr Paula, a Greek specialist, in private correspondence with the author.
15 Bauer, Arnt, Gingrich, A Lexicon of NT Greek and Early Christian Literature.
16 Jones, James, *Jesus and the Earth*, 2003, p.17.

PART 3   THE USE OF THE LAND'S RESOURCES

Wetlands or marshes have been described as the 'lungs of the earth'. Or perhaps 'the kidneys' since they purify the waters of earth. Yet by 1993 over half the wetlands of the world had been drained to provide building land or land for cultivating and grazing. In 2004 when the tsunami hit South-east Asia, it was noticeable that where the mangrove swamps had not been cleared, the waves were reduced and the damage was considerably less than where they had been drained[1].

In Southwest Uganda, where I was at school as a child, I remember cold misty mornings, fertile hillsides and valleys filled with marshes. But since then about 58% of these marshes have been drained to provide land for agriculture and dairy farming for the increasing population in the area. A recent survey[2] asked the local population what effects this has had on the area. The local inhabitants had noticed the following effects:

- To begin with the reclaimed land produced abundant crops, which provided needed money, but after a time the soil often became acid and needed artificial fertilisation, which reduced the profit.
- Wells which had been dug at the borders of the marshes before the land was reclaimed and had produced abundant clear water were now insufficient if large amounts of water were required for ceremonies, when large quantities of food and drink were needed. Often the water became muddy, resulting in stomach problems and the need to buy expensive medicines.
- Heavy rains often made paths impassable and journeys that used to take 30 minutes by boat could now take two hours.
- Fish which had provided needed protein and money through sales for the local people are much harder to find - obviously they do not survive in the reclaimed lands but even in the few remaining marshes, they are scarce.
- The *sitatunga*, or water antelope, which used to be hunted had now completely disappeared.
- Raw materials for building and traditional crafts are harder to find.
- Many medicinal herbs have been lost.

- Crowned cranes, (golden crested) the national bird of Uganda, need marshland to nest in and they have been reduced in number.
- There is now an unpredictable local climate, making it hard to know when to plant. The morning mists usually clear by 7am, where they used to last until 11.30am or later, and often there are 8 hours of heat, from 8am - 4pm, making cultivation much harder. Long dry periods also dry the soil making it much harder to dig.
- These dry periods are now punctuated by heavy rains, causing destructive floods and landslides which destroy crops and homes.

There may be other consequences not yet apparent.

As a result of this and other studies, the Uganda Government now has a policy to protect the remaining marshlands and even in some cases to allow drained land to return to its former condition. Yet with Uganda's population expected to treble by the year 2050, pressure to drain remaining marshes for agricultural purposes remains.

In Rwanda, too, the Government has been discovering the benefits of protecting wetlands. Since Independence in 1962, these wetlands have been steadily drained to provide needed agricultural land for the increasing population. The Rugezi Wetland[3] which ends in the Virunga National Park is one of the head waters of the Nile. In 1979 it was decided to drain the Lake at the other end of the Wetland, one of the actual sources of the Nile, by blasting a hole through the rock formation which formed a natural dam so as to grow sunflowers commercially. The result was disastrous. Lakes Burera and Ruhondo, the source of Rwanda's hydroelectic scheme, became dangerously low and too much water flowed into the neighbouring valley creating problems for the burgeoning tea industry there. After a few years the hole was again dammed and the wetland started to recover but much land, particularly in the north had been lost to agriculture.

By 2000 only half of the swamp remained in its natural state and the water level in the nearby Lakes Ruhondo and Burera had reached a record low creating a crisis in electricity for the whole country. In 2005, the electricity company dug a deep channel across the centre of the swamp, hoping that this would cause the water levels to rise. In fact it drained the wetland still further.

Later that same year, the Rwanda Government signed the Ramsar Convention on Wetlands and started taking active steps to regenerate some of the wetlands in the country. In 2006, the Rugezi Wetland was declared a Wetland of International Importance. Terracing on the hillsides proved four times more productive than the reclaimed land from the marshes. Papyrus has again started growing (though still threatened) and rare birds which had disappeared have returned. By 2009, women were again harvesting reeds for handcrafts, men were fishing and hunting as before and canoes were taking passengers across the swamps once more. In October 2010 a global green award was given to Rwanda for work on the Rugezi Wetlands.

There are high hopes that the beauty of the area will attract tourists as the bio-diversity returns, providing needed income for the area. A hopeful start has been made in reversing the trend of decades and the wetland is once more fulfilling its role in the environment, regulating the flood-waters, retaining water for times of drought and filtering the water which had been carrying silt out of the area.

We have seen above how marsh reduction has altered a local climate system. Since the industrial revolution and the discovery of oil at the turn of the 18th century, climate has been changing on a global scale. This has largely been caused by increased carbon dioxide in the atmosphere from burning irreplaceable fossil fuels like coal, gas and oil, and methane from intensive livestock farming. This increase of greenhouse gases (which are naturally occurring and needed in smaller amounts) has caused more of the sun's radiation to be trapped within the earth's atmosphere, leading to global warming. This has become increasingly apparent in the last 50 years with the following effects:

- Increased mean temperatures in the world
- Rise in the sea level in the world
- Melting of icecaps and glaciers
- Increase in the frequency and intensity of floods, storms and drought

Unless we take action fast to reduce our consumption of fossil fuels then the above effects will continue, with damage to local ecosystems and extinction of many species of animals and plants. While there will be an increased need for water to save failing crops during droughts, rising sea levels will threaten many major cities in the world.

The Government of Rwanda has taken steps to stop the cutting down of trees and burning of charcoal, which helps the environment but at the same time has made life even harder for the really poor who depend on trees for their fuel. The Government has also banned the use of non-bio-degradeable plastic bags. As a result, Kigali has been declared the cleanest city in Africa.

BIBLE STUDY 3.1   THE BIBLE AND THE USE OF THE WORLD'S RESOURCES

<u>Starter Question</u>

What can we do at a local level to live more sustainably? Is sustainable living only a problem for governments or can individuals make a difference?

1   Consider what God put in the Garden of Eden. What aesthetic as well as practical resources was Adam asked to care for?

Genesis 2:9

Genesis 2:10

Genesis 2:12

<u>Note:</u>
- There were beautiful trees as well as fruitful ones
- There was a water system to be managed
- There was mineral wealth to be mined

However in **Genesis 1:29** God only allowed them to have a vegetarian diet, so that fishing and hunting would probably not have been part of their remit. It was only after the Flood that meat was allowed to be eaten. (**Genesis 9:3-4**) According to Food and Agriculture Organisation (FAO) of the United Nations, intensive farming of meat today causes 18% of all greenhouse gases[4]. Besides being often cruel to the animals, over 1/3 of all arable land is used in intensive farming and it is responsible for some pesticide pollution of water and for deforestation especially in South America. As a result, many Christians today believe that they should return to the creation (vegetarian) diet or at least use meat as a rare treat. However, small scale farming with integration of

37

crops and livestock has been shown to be beneficial to soil and farmers.[5] There are also lands throughout the world which are unsuitable for growing grain and where farming of livestock is a useful way of using the land.

In **Job 28** there is a fascinating description of mining and manufacturing, as well as water management, but where, Job asks, is wisdom to be found? (**Job 28:12-15, 23, 28**)

Once the people of Israel entered the Promised Land, several laws were given indicating how God wanted the land used.

2   What can we learn from the following verses about the use of the world's resources?

Exodus 20:8-11

Exodus 23:10-11

Leviticus 19:9-10; 23:22

Leviticus 19:23-25

Leviticus 25:2-7

Proverbs 12:10

Isaiah 28:24-26

Note:
- The Sabbath was a day of rest not only for the household but also for the working animals.
- Newly planted trees need time to mature before they are harvested

- The land needed a regular rest, lying fallow for a year, providing food not only for the poor but also for the wild creatures, suggesting that we ought to care for them regardless of need.
- Fields were not to be over-harvested but crops were to be left for the poor.
- The skill to produce crops is God-given.

One way we can consider protecting the resources of God's earth is to renounce "Consumerism". Part of the global problem is an emphasis on material goods which are often cheap and of poor quality and which add nothing of value to one's lifestyle. Before buying anything one ought to ask questions like:
- Do I really need this?
- How well made is it and how long will it last?
- What resources and energy have been used to make it?
- How can I re-use or recycle this once I have finished with it?

According to my brother, John Guillebaud, this is summarised as the hierarchy of 5 R's of environmental care, which we need to remember. Many of these still happen automatically in countries like Rwanda, though as wealth increases, they are being often ignored there, as they are largely in the West:

REFUSE to use things unnecessarily (e.g., walk or cycle rather than drive).

REDUCE i.e., efficient use of needed resources (e.g., use fuel efficient stoves for cooking).

RE-USE (bags, bottles, tins etc.)

REPAIR wherever possible (even if that is more expensive than buying a new one!)

RECYCLE (e.g., making lamps out of small tin cans, often found in Rwandan markets).

Discussion Questions

1 Is it wrong to mine for gold and precious jewels? How can mining be done in a way that does not damage the environment?

2 Do you think that Adam made pretty gardens in Eden? What is the benefit of caring for our surroundings and making sure they are clean and tidy as well as pretty?

3 Letting the land lie fallow is both a Biblical principle and good agricultural practice, but does this involve issues of faith and trust for God to provide for our needs during the fallow time?

4 How can we reduce consumerism in our situation?

BIBLE STUDY 3.2   __POPULATION__

Starter Question

God commanded his creation to 'fill' the earth. What do you think does God mean by full, and when is the Earth overfilled?

When people were all hunter-gatherers, food supply was unpredictable and the whole world human population was probably a few million. About 10,000 years ago people began to settle and to farm the land. Food supplies became more stable and the population began to rise - to about 250 million in 1AD and 461 million by 1500AD[6] rising to its first billion by 1800AD[7] But with the discovery of oil, leading to ease of travel, and the start of the Industrial Revolution, populations rose rapidly so that by 1900 there were 1.6 billion in the world. By 1950 this figure had risen to 2.5 billion[8] and the 3rd billion by 1960[9]. With the rise of modern medicine and improving hygiene, there was a still more rapid increase: 4 billion in 1975, 5 billion in 1987 and 6 billion in 1999[9]. Today, in 2010, the world population is approaching 7 billion[10]. It is projected to rise to 9.4 billion by 2050[9], increasing by 85 million a year - ten times the population of Rwanda every year! (Graph below [11])

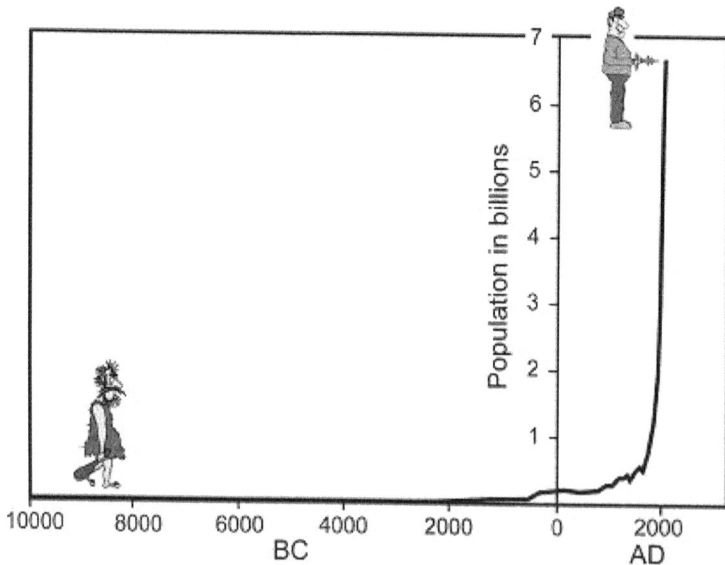

The population of Rwanda is about 375 people per sq km compared with an average of 33 per sq km elsewhere in Africa.[12] In 1950 the population was about 2.1 million rising to 8.1 million by 2002[13] and 9.9 by the middle of 2009[11]. In other words, the decimation of the population caused by the genocide of 1994 had been more than restored, partly by immigration but more worryingly by new births. If the annual growth rate of population of 2.8% in 2009 persists, the population is projected to rise to about 14.5 million by 2020[10], i.e., about 50% more than in 2009!

In 2007, the Government of Rwanda started encouraging people to limit their families to 2 or 3, but to a people who for generations had had large families to counter ravages of death by sickness and famine, this is not an easy message. Many say, "An extra child is another pair of hands to help in the field, and to care for me in my old age." Even amongst the educated, urban middle class, numerous children are still a source of pride. The prevailing view is that there is no problem if you can afford to have more children.

As we have seen, the pressure of human population led to the draining of the wetlands of South Western Uganda and northern Rwanda with a resulting detrimental effect on the environment.

Is it right to limit the size of one's family? Conversely, is it right to continue to produce large families even though the pressure on land is destroying the environment? On 13 December 2009 during the Copenhagen conference on climate change the Archbishop of Canterbury preached on casting out fear and acting for the sake of love. He said that "we cannot show the right kind of love for our fellow-humans unless we also work at keeping the earth as a place that is a secure home for all people for future generations." [14] On 18th March 2010 the Public Affairs Commission of the General Synod of the Anglican Church of Australia produced a discussion paper on population issues in which they said "unless we take account of the needs of future

life on Earth, there is a case that we break the eighth commandment —
"Thou shalt not steal"."[14] ie stealing both from poorer nations and from
future generations.

In Rwanda the two largest groups of Christians (the Roman Catholics
and the Pentecostals) as well as many other individual Christians, say
that family planning is wrong; that children are a blessing from God and
that we should trust him for the size of the family. Is this faith or
fatalism? Are our decisions on family size related to stewardship of the
earth's resources?

1   What does the Bible say? Is there a difference in what God said to
    the animals and birds and in what he said to the humans?
Genesis 1:22

Genesis 1:28

Genesis 9:1

Note:
*   The command to the animals came first before mankind was told to
    fill the earth. If the environment is destroyed this means that the
    animals cannot fulfil this first command. There is no indication that
    God wanted either to impede the development of the other - he
    wanted both to flourish.
*   Sin entered the world after this command was given. As a result
    everything was affected and human greed and selfishness have
    implications for population growth.
*   Yet the same command, to fill the earth, was given to Noah after sin
    entered the world. At that stage, according to the Bible, there were
    only 8 people on earth: perhaps the different situation in the world
    today means that we should view this command differently.

In Rwanda land is generally equally divided among all the children after the death of the father, meaning that each child often has an unsustainably small piece of land. It is often said that land hunger was one of the underlying causes of the genocide of 1994. Environmentalists and politicians warn that, as the sea rises through climate change and floods destroy more land, there will be millions of environmental refugees bringing pressure on ever decreasing areas of land.

2   What happened between Lot and Abraham when the land was too small for all their livestock? (**Genesis 13:6-7**)

With the rising world population, surely it makes sense to make contraceptives available to all who want to use them. Many Christians say that the story of Onan in **Genesis 38:1-11**, shows that God is against preventing births, but this story is in the context of Levirate marriages, which was God's provision for Israel to ensure that land remained within the family. Also Onan deliberately broke his promise to his father to raise a child for his older brother.

3   a   What provision is made to allow the land of a man who has died childless to continue in his family? (**Deuteronomy 25:5-6**)

   b   What if he died leaving only daughters? (**Numbers 27:1-7**)

   c   Why do you think that God was angry with Onan? (**Genesis 38:9-10**)

4   Other passages are also used by some Christians to say that they must leave the size of their family to God. Do these verses really show that God is against family planning?
1 Samuel 1:19-20

Psalm 139:15-16

Jeremiah 1:5

Other Christians say that sexual intercourse should be solely for the purpose of reproduction.

5   What do the following verses say?
Genesis 2:24

Malachi 2:15 (NIV)

1 Corinthians 7:5

Scientists have shown that the female clitoris has no function in the reproductive process except to give the woman pleasure during sexual intercourse. It would seem, therefore, that God intended that sexual intercourse should be as much a pleasurable experience for both husband and wife, as for the purpose of reproduction. Indeed, some Christians would say that as their bodies are joined, so their spirits are joined with God in an act of worship.[15]

The Hebrew word translated 'cleave' or 'be united' in **Genesis 2:24** has the same root as 'glue'. The sex act is intended to continue throughout marriage, strengthening the bond of friendship and should be a source of comfort and support, making the two one in every sense of the word.

45

Some Christians teach that sexual intercourse only started after Adam and Eve sinned and is therefore evil and dirty. Much harm has been done by this sort of thinking and it is contrary to the Bible which teaches that it is a great gift of God. One whole book, the Song of Solomon, can be read as celebrating to the joys of sex! Yet the Bible does strongly teach that it should only be practised within the covenant of marriage. All else is sin and can indeed bring much harm.

Poverty can often be made worse by having more children than the family can properly care for. Now that contraception is readily available, it could be regarded as good stewardship to limit the size of family. In the 1970's a Rwandan Christian said to my father, *"Surely God intended the Christian home to be like a re-creation of the Garden of Eden, inhabited by a man and a woman who love God first and also each other. What if the little garden of Eden of this married Christian couple is about to be destroyed because there are more children than can properly be cared for? Surely family planning is right so that the couple can fulfil God's main purpose in marriage - the lovemaking that glues the relationship together - without destroying their garden of Eden."*

Discussion Questions
1   Is the story of Onan about family planning or obedience to God's plan for the inheritance of land?
2   Does the fact that there is no verse in the New Testament contradicting the creation command to fill the earth mean that it is still valid? What other commands in the Old Testament can you think of which have never been clearly cancelled but which people do not consider binding today?
3   Are contraceptives a gift of God for the sensible use of mankind within marriage (to preserve that 'little garden of Eden') or an encouragement to promiscuity?
4   What effect has the spiralling human population growth on the rest of creation? Does this fulfil God's will?

Notes on Part 3:

1   Asian Wetland Symposium, 9th February 2005, www.riverbasin.org
2   Barakagira, Alex and Eliezer Kateyo, 2008, *Impacts of Wetland Drainage on Domestic Water Supplies and People's livelihoods in Kabale District, Uganda*, http://dlcvm.dlib.indiana.edu/archive
3   Hategekimana, Sylvere and Emmanuel Twarabamenye, *The Impact of Wetlands degradation on water resources management in Rwanda: the case of Rugezi Swamp*, http://www.irst.ac.rw/IMG/pdf/Paper_for_V_International_Symposium_on_En_Hydrology1.pdf
4   Article, "Livestock impacts on the Environment", 2006, www.fao.org/ag/magazine .
5   Article, "Why Livestock Matter", 2007, International Livestock Research Institute, www.ilri.org
6   Livvi-Bacci, M., 2001, *A Concise History of World Populatiom*, 3rd Edn, pp. 24-28, as quoted by Hodson, Martin and Margot, *Cherishing the Earth*, 2008, p.63.
7   World Population Video, http://www.populationeducation.org.
8   Livvi-Bacci , 2001, as quoted by Hodson, 2008, p.64.
9   http://www.populationeducation.org World Population video.
10 World Population, www.geohive.com .
11 Image courtesy of Professor Bob White, Cambridge
12 World Population Data Sheet 2009, www.prb.org.
13 Rwanda, Population, Health and Human Well-being, www.earthtrends.wri.org.
14 www.anglican.org.au/Web/Website.nsf/content/ A_Discussion_Paper_on_Population_Issues,_prepared_by_the_P ublic_Affairs_Commission_of_the_General_Synod_of_the_Angli can_Church_of_Australia._March_2010
15 Southern, Jill, 2006, *Sex - God's Truth*, pp. 13-15

PART 4   OVERVIEW OF WORLDVIEWS

In post-modern thinking everything has become relativistic, and to talk in absolute terms is suspect, particularly with regard to ethical issues. So much depends on how we view the world, both with regard to moral issues and the use of technology. Although there are many ways of interpreting worldviews, there are basically only three main ones: the view that everything has a physical cause, the view that the spirits are behind everything, or the Biblical view which shows that both physical and spiritual are important. All other views are variations on these three basic ones.

In 2008, I listened to a series of talks by Dennis Tongoi, General Secretary of CMS-Africa, who used to work for Navigators (an international Christian discipling organisation). He was puzzled by the fact that, however well discipled in the Bible young Kenyan Christians were, when they went into the realm of commerce or politics they often became as corrupt as any. He decided that it was a problem of worldview and is happy to endorse an initiative developed in 1979 between Food for the Hungry and the Harvest Foundation called the Samaritan Strategy which "encourages, prepares and equips churches around the globe with a Biblical worldview to carry out wholistic ministry in their communities." He spoke about three basic worldviews: the humanist, the traditional or the Biblical.

Renée Schudel, was a missionary with Youth with a Mission in Liberia and has since worked in reconciliation in Rwanda and South Africa. She also recognised that people's established ways of thinking often led to total misunderstandings among them. She has written a book on worldviews called *Changed Minds, Changed Lives*[1], in which she describes three different worldviews: the secular, the animist or the Biblical.

Alistair Petrie writes, "The way we think affects the way we live, act and interact with the rest of creation. Surely this is part of what lies behind

Paul's thinking in Romans 12:2 and Philippians 2:1-5 in exhorting us to allow our minds to be transformed, and to think like Christ."[2] He points out that Zechariah 9:13 highlights a conflict between the sons of Greece and the sons of Zion. Greek thinking has been extremely influential in our world and in Western understanding of Christianity. It was through Greek philosophers that the humanist viewpoint became strong, the view that "whatever does not breathe, taught Aristotle, has no intelligence, will or desire. Spirit, if it exists at all, is different and apart from matter and human life."[3]

Equally, Eastern mystical religions also had an influence on Greek thought and gnostic thinking with its dualism of body and spirit. Gnostics divide everything into spiritual things which are of the light and good, or material things which are dark and evil. So, as Petrie says, the challenge of Zechariah remains: "Am I a child of Greece or a child of Zion?"[4] In other words, are my worldviews Biblical or have I been influenced by secular or animist thinking? So often our reading of Scripture is influenced by our worldview. As we have already seen, the Bible speaks of creation worshipping God and this is sometimes hard to visualize. Petrie says, "When we read that Jesus spoke directly to the winds of the storm and that they obeyed him, our human thinking tells us that winds and storms have no life of their own, so how could they hear, understand or obey Jesus? We relegate much of Scripture to superstition. Sometimes we go so far as to demythologize it, stripping it of 'myth' so we can believe it."[5] If creation can worship the Lord, why wouldn't it hear Jesus?

So what is a worldview? According to Samaritan Strategy, it is "like a pair of glasses. It determines what we see, not what is there to be seen. Many of us wear glasses. What happens when you take them off? The world looks a little different. Worldview is like a set of glasses for the

49

mind. Everyone has these glasses on their mind, and the lenses in them have been set by culture. We all have a worldview, a framework by which we interpret reality."[6]

Though there may be dozens of individual worldviews they all basically fall into one of three general worldviews and they affect our whole way of thinking:

1   The secular or humanist worldview

This view is basically physical or materialistic. The only reality is what we can see, touch, hear, or feel. There is no room for anything to do with God or spirits - they are an illusion. Although the rise of modern science came out of Christian thinking, and many top scientists today are Christians; the scientific method essentially operates within the physical realm.

Renée Schudel says that "with scientific reasoning as its basis, the secular worldview's question to a problem is *how and what.* What has occurred? How has it occurred and what can we do to make it happen again, or to stop it from ever happening again?"[7] From questions like these, the scientific method developed. It is purely physical in its scope, seeking to explain how the universe works. But the way that scientific discoveries are used obviously depends on the user. Nuclear science has led to the nuclear bomb but also to cures for cancer, relatively clean electricity and many other benefits.

This worldview is also essentially anthropocentric - man and his ideas are central to the world. Time is a valuable resource to be used to the full and saved by time-saving devices. Everything has to be planned for and the future is what is important.   Youth and energy are what is important and the elderly are frequently regarded as a nuisance. The secular worldview considers poverty as something to be fixed. The structures of society must be unjust to allow poverty, or perhaps the person in poverty is to be blamed for not working hard enough. Either way, poverty can become history if we all put our minds to it.

2   The animist or traditional worldview

This view holds that there is a spiritual reason for everything. There is no point in trying to improve life or develop the world because everything is determined by the spirits, which are beyond our control. Hinduism, Buddhism, Islam and many other religions grew out of this way of thinking. "Fatalism is the end result of believing that spirits ae in control. There is no point in trying to change things or improve things because the spirits will decide what happens anyway."[8]

In this worldview, the questions are *who and why*? Which spirit is behind my problem and which of my enemies influenced that spirit. This leads to the wearing of charms, or other superstitions to try to influence the spirits.[9] Even the Bible can be used as a fetish - with some people sleeping with it under the pillow for protection.

Lest we think this is only an African or Eastern way of thinking, I remember being in a meeting in Norwich, England, when this question was addressed and many Christians produced rabbit's feet, lucky beans, or St Christopher's medals which they were carrying for protection.

Nature is to be feared and changes in the environment are likely to be resisted because they might offend the spirits. In this worldview, the past is what is important. Old people are valued for their wisdom. The future is too uncertain to be considered and to plan ahead is to ask for trouble from the spirits. Often, in Rwanda, mothers would arrive at hospital to give birth bringing nothing for the coming child. That would be to tempt providence. Even in the West, this attitude underlies many of our superstitions. How often do people touch wood or cross their fingers, when speaking of the future, habits which have their origin in appeasing spirits?

Someone with this worldview often believes that he is trapped in poverty and there is no way out. Poverty is caused by the spirits who must be angry with the poor person. They need to be appeased but even so there is no way out. Some people will always be rich and others poor. That is the way the world is.

3   The Biblical worldview recognises both physical and spiritual

The Bible teaches that there is only one God, who is spirit, yet at the incarnation, He became man in Jesus Christ. When God created man he breathed his life into us so that we are both physical and spiritual beings, made in his likeness. His Holy Spirit hovered over the waters as the world was created and, as we have seen, he is deeply involved in all of creation. He created all things, both the physical world and the spiritual realm.

There are physical reasons for things that happen but also spiritual reasons. In the Biblical worldview we need to exercise spiritual discernment to discover what is going on. It may be that there is a purely physical reason for my sickness, such as drinking contaminated water, or there may be a spiritual reason for it as Job discovered, or possibly both. The question we need to ask is, *what can I learn from this event?*

People with a Biblical worldview see the truths discovered by science as enhancing their picture of God, but understand that science can never describe all there is in the world since it is primarily concerned with the physical. Science answers the question *"how?"* whereas the Bible answers the question *"what for?"* The Bible shows that the world, including mankind, was created to display God's glory.

Having said that, I am aware that there are some Christians who think that Science has now replaced God in many people's minds and they are suspicious of any answers backed up by scientific reasoning. We need to be alert to this danger and careful to run all scientific conclusions through the lens of the Bible. Remember that science can be considered as discovering what God already knew, since He is the creator of all things. At the same time, we need to recognise that the Bible, written more than two thousand years ago cannot be expected to describe things in the detailed way that modern science does.

The whole earth is the Lord's and we need to care for it as God's stewards. Causes of poverty are often man-made and yet Jesus said "The poor you will always have with you." (John 12:8) Poverty spoils the harmony of God's world and He is against those who exploit the poor, so we need to fight poverty and care for those who are disadvantaged. How we view the world has a direct impact on our approach to the environment.

Mrs Debby Thomas of Evangelical Friends Mission in Rwanda has been involved in Discipling for Development over the past few years. As part of her training, she visited one community in Uganda where the people in poverty were waiting for others to come and solve their problems of poverty, poor water and bad crops. Yet about 5 km away was another community, which had been trained in Discipling for Development; they had dug wells, their crops were flourishing and there were several thriving churches in the area. Her experiences in Uganda led her to start a Discipling for Development programme in Rwanda. This involves training people to look at their worldviews and seeing how developing a Biblical worldview can actually change communities and the way the environment is affected.

Discipling for Development came out of Mission: Moving Mountains, a branch of the Navigators. In 1979 Dick and Marilyn Patterson had been working with Navigators for some years. They perceived that although this system of Bible Discipling seemed to help urban, educated Christians, it made no impact on rural communities. They started training local community leaders in Mbale, Uganda, and soon found that they needed to help people to change their whole worldview. Instead of waiting for others to tell them what to do, or to give them handouts to start projects that often went nowhere, their students learnt to look at their own resources and how to solve their own problems.

In 2009, 60 entire communities in Uganda are being transformed and work has been started in 30 more. Their work has attracted the attention of the Ugandan Government who recommend donor parties to work through them rather than starting income generating projects on their own. "Sustainable change is readily apparent in things like wells that provide clean drinking water, vibrant new churches and improved agriculture techniques. It is also apparent in the new skills leaders have developed, such as solving problems together, using the community's own resources, and trusting God as he continues to move their hearts toward him."[10]

In Kigali, Debby has found that community leaders are looking at the barriers to development and asking what it is that holds them in poverty. As their worldview becomes more Biblical, they look at their circumstances in a different way. For example, at a recent training session, when they were asked what their resources were, they came up with two pages of answers instead of taking refuge in poverty. They have found that changing their worldview has led to a change of attitude to their environment.

BIBLE STUDY 4.1   A BIBLICAL WORLDVIEW

Starter Question

Is the distrust of science expressed by many Christians, particularly with regard to global warming, connected to their worldview?

1   **Proverbs 23:7 (KJV)** says "As a man thinketh so he is." (the Hebrew is obscure and other versions say different things). What do the following verses say about our minds?

Romans 12:2

2 Corinthians 10:5

Philippians 2:5

2   In the familiar story of the feeding of the 5000, (**Mark 6:30-44**) how does Jesus challenge the worldview of his disciples? (see especially **6:35-41**)

3   How does Jesus demonstrate his authority over nature in the following passages?

Mark 5:35-43

Mark 6:47-52

Mark 11:20-23

4   He gave authority to his disciples to do what?

Matthew 10:1

Mark 16:15-18

5   What does God say about man in **Genesis 1:26**?

Part of being created in God's image is that like him we have creativity and he intends us to use our creativity to solve our problems. This is what Debby Thomas has been finding as she studies Discipling for Development. People are using their minds to solve problems in ways she would never have thought about but as they pray, God helps them use their resources in new ways. God has created us with minds. He has created a world filled with things to care for and use. The problem is that since the industrial revolution, we have become dependent on oil and coal and only recently have started to look beyond them for sources of energy.

As people have been considering these different worldviews in the light of the Bible, whether in Uganda or Rwanda, so mindsets have altered and attitudes to problems have changed. Christians in the West also need to have their mindsets changed as we seek to do God's will in our world. Climate change can be tackled if we allow our God to help us think creatively about the issues.

Greenhouse gases do not respect national boundaries and one way we need to tackle climate change is by developing a world where nations truly cooperate to reduce their emissions.

6   What does the Bible say about Christians?
Matthew 5:13

John 17:22

Ephesians 4:3

Discussion Questions

1 How does the Bible challenge:
  - the humanistic worldview?
  - the animistic worldview?
2 How can we be more creative in our approach to the environment?
3 What can we do as Christians to demonstrate unity and be salt in our community with regard to the environment?

Notes on Part 4:

1 Schudel, Renée, *Changed Minds, Changed Lives,* The Whole Person Health Trust, London, 2004.
2 Petrie, Alistair, *Releasing Heaven on Earth*, 2000, p. 109.
3 Ibid., p. 111.
4 Ibid., p. 110.
5 Ibid., p. 111.
6 Samaritan Strategy Publicity pamphlet.
7 Schudel, Renée, *Changed Minds, Changed Lives*, 2004, p. 18.
8 Ibid., p 19.
9 Ibid.
10 Mentoring Projects, Uganda.
  www.navigators.org/us/ministries/movingmountains.

PART 5

A NEW HEAVEN AND A NEW EARTH

This is an area which I approach with some trepidation since I am aware that it is a matter of some controversy amongst Christians. My entire thinking on the subject has undergone a radical transformation in the last year or so since I began to consider the whole area of conservation.

The first challenge was to my understanding of the word 'new'. The Bible uses two Greek words: *Neos* which usually means new or young and *kainos* which usually means new, fresh, recent, or newly made[1]. While there is a lot of overlap of the two words in the New Testament, what struck me was that the same word *kainos* was used when referring to a new heaven and a new earth (**2 Peter 3:13, Revelation 21:1**), and also for redeemed Christians - we are a new creation (**2 Corinthians 5:17, Ephesians 4:24**) and when God says "I will make all things new" (**Revelation 21:5**). However, in **Colossians 3:10**, it is the word *neos* which is used, also referring to our new nature so we should not place too much emphasis on the choice of word but rather on the concept of newness. When we become Christians, our old nature dies and we are new in the eyes of God, in the same way, is it possible that when the time is right, all that is evil in this world will die and we will be left in a transformed and new earth?

Then came the challenge of the Greek word, *parousia,* which is used in **1 Thessalonians 4:15** for the coming of the Lord Jesus. Often, when I go to visit a Parish in Rwanda, the choir will come to meet me at the main road and will return with me, singing along the way. In New Testament times, when a king visited a city, a herald would first announce his imminent coming, the citizens would meet him some distance away and would return with him, singing his praises along the way. His actual presence in the city, beside them is the *parousia.* In **1 Thessalonians 4:17**, where it talks about Christians on earth meeting the Lord in the air, it could be this practice that is being referred to and that they will return with him to the earth and be in his presence there. **2 Thessalonians 2:1** also speaks of the Christians assembling to meet him.

Finally, a friend really startled me when he pointed out that in **Matthew 24:40-41** when Jesus is talking about two men walking in the field and two women grinding at the mill, "one will be taken and the other left" it does not say which will be taken! Suddenly, all my thinking about the end times was turned on its head. Could it be that instead of the righteous being taken away in the Rapture as so many Christians think, that it will be the sinners taken for judgement?

Like many other Christians I had assumed that we go to heaven, a rather hazy place but in the presence of God, when we die. I also believed that heaven and earth as we know them would be destroyed by fire (**2 Peter 3:10**). I had been bothered by the covenant that God made with Noah, that never again would all living creatures be destroyed (**Genesis 8:21-22**) but had explained that by the extra words added in **Genesis 9:11-15** that they would not be destroyed by flood, rather they would be destroyed by fire (**2 Peter 3:10**). After that there would be a new heaven and new earth, with heaven being on earth since God would live with his people on earth, (**Revelation 21:1-3**) and there would be no more pain or sorrow of separation or sin (**Revelation 21:4,27**) - a concept rather hard to imagine but delightful to contemplate.

The meaning of the Greek in the last sentence of **2 Peter 3:10** is by no means clear and we must be cautious how we interpret it but David Wilkinson says "the most attractive solution seems to be to take the words simply as 'the earth and everything in it will be found' in the sense of will be made manifest before God and his judgement. Thus the NIV is helpful in its translation of *will be laid bare*."[2] He concludes that although there will be cataclysmic events when God intervenes in judgement just as there was at the time of the Flood there is no justification for saying that the earth will be destroyed as it was not in the Flood. (p. 256) Later in the same book, commenting on **Revelation 21:1-8** he asks "What does it mean for the first heaven and earth to pass away? Is God going to destroy this Universe and make a new one? Is he going to start all over again? The problem with this is, what was the point of the first creation in the first place and will God really be defeated by sin to the extent that he has to scrap the lot and start again? As in the interpretation of **2 Peter 3:3-13**, most recent scholars see an image here of transformation rather than destruction."[3] In other words the fire referred to in **2 Peter 3:10** is the refining fire of judgement rather than the destruction I and so many other Christians had thought.

Bishop Tom Wright's book, "Surprised by Hope"[4] confirms this understanding of transformation rather than the destruction of earth and heaven. To my surprise, I also found that, "From the earliest times, right up until the nineteenth century, the majority of Christians believed that God's plans for the earth were more about continuity than discontinuity, more about a hopeful future than destruction."[5] Let us look at some examples:

"Since men really exist, their renewal must be something that really exists - not a departure into nothingness, but an actual advance in the real world. It is not the substance or essence of creation that is brought to an end, for He who established it is true and constant, but the 'fashion of this world passeth away', that is to say, those aspects in which transgression had been committed." (Ireneaus,130-200 AD)[6]

"Paul does not mean that all creatures will be partakers of the same glory with the sons of God, but that they will share in their own manner in the better state...... It is neither expedient nor right for us to inquire with greater curiosity into the perfection which will be evidenced by beasts, plants and metals." (John Calvin, commenting on **Romans 8:21**).[7] He also said "God will restore the present fallen world to a perfect condition."

"No rage will be found in any creature, no fierceness or thirst for blood. So far from it that 'the wolf shall dwell with the lamb' (**Isaiah 11:6-9**). As a recompense for what they once suffered ... they shall enjoy happiness suited to their state, without interruption and without end." (John Wesley, Sermons, Vol 11)[8]

The Anglican refrain says "Glory to the Father, the Son and the Holy Spirit. As it was in the beginning, is now and ever shall be, world without end. Amen"[9] which seems to imply that the world shall not end. (c.f. **Ephesians 3:21**)

It is only in the last 200 years, since the start of the Industrial Revolution when many people left the countryside to live in cities, that the idea of the destruction of the earth has become prevalent. Indeed, a reason often given for not getting involved in environmental issues, is that if Jesus is to return soon and the earth is to be destroyed, why seek to restore it? Some go even further and say that the quicker the earth is destroyed, the sooner the Lord Jesus will return!

If the same reasoning were to be applied to the human body, everyone would be appalled! Yet we must all die one day. Nothing is as certain. Why then care for the body? Why not let it decay as soon as possible?

Whatever happens to the earth at the time of the Lord's return, one thing is clear. It was created, in love by God, who continues to care for it. Surely as Christians we can do no less.

BIBLE STUDY 5.1   <u>END TIMES AND ECOLOGY</u>

<u>Starter Question</u>

Consider these two statements by leading Christians of the past:

"If I knew that the world was going to end tomorrow, I'd plant a tree." (Martin Luther, 1483-1546)

"You don't polish the brass on a sinking ship." (Dwight Moody, 1837-1899)

Which most accurately sums up your thinking? Why? Is there merit in the opposite statement? Are the times they lived in relevant to their thinking?

I have looked at all the verses in the Old Testament which speak about an end. Nowhere have I seen it said that the earth will end! However, God will judge the inhabitants of the land for their sin. Yet, just as in the days of Noah, when God saved a remnant, both of man and of all living creatures, so in the last days there will also be a remnant. During the time of exile, too, God saved a remnant, not in Jerusalem but in Babylon, where they were told to put down roots where they were and seek the good of their captors, so that they too might be blessed and eventually return to their land. (**Jeremiah 29:5-7**) The good news is that God has always saved a remnant even in his severest judgements, and it seems that the last days will be no different.

1   What hope can you find in these verses?
Proverbs 23:18

Jeremiah 29:11-14

<u>Note:</u>
- However grim the time God always seems to promise hope for the future.

62

2   The classic picture of the end times in the Old Testament can be found in the following verses. They are surprisingly physical. You might like to list all the evidence that points to an earth restored to its former perfection.

Isaiah 2:2-4

Isaiah 11:6-9

Isaiah 13:10-13

Amos 8:9-10

Note:
- The picture here is of a tranquil earth, no more wars and everything dwelling together in harmony, yet still a very 'earthy' earth.
- Yet there is also a picture of cataclysmic environmental disturbance.
- Judgement shall be on the inhabitants but in the end there will be an earth that was as God originally intended it to be.

3   This same picture of cataclysmic environmental disturbance is repeated in the New Testament. What do these verses indicate?

Matthew 24:29

Matthew 24:35 (compare with **Psalm 119:89-90**)

2 Peter 3:7

2 Peter 3:10

Revelation 6:12-14

Revelation 21:1

4   If you only concentrated on these verses, the natural conclusion would be that heaven and earth will be destroyed. Yet what do the following verses indicate?
Romans 8:19-20

1 Corinthians 15:24

2 Thessalonians 2:8

Revelation 11:15

Note:
*   One of Christ's tasks on his return is to destroy every ruler and authority which denies God's rule. This is generally taken to mean spiritual powers, which nevertheless have real power on earth.

Discussion Questions
1   What place does the non-human creation play in the new creation?
2   In what way is all creation waiting for the liberation of humankind? **(Romans 8:19-20)**
3   What will the second coming of the Lord Jesus achieve on earth?

BIBLE STUDY 5.2   **THE RETURN OF CHRIST**

Starter Question
What do you think will happen when we die or at the return of Christ?

There are over 300 references in the New Testament to the return of Christ. This is about the only thing that Christians totally agree about with regard to the end times - that he will return! When, how and what will happen are all causes for debate. It is really important that we are willing to agree to differ over these issues. However important they are, they are not salvation issues, but we should not be frightened of discussing them to see what we can learn about our responsibilities in God's world.

There are three Greek words used of the return of Jesus Christ.

1   *parousia* or coming. This indicates the coming of the Lord to be present with his people for ever. This is the word used in the following verses, what is the emphasis in them?
Matthew 24:37- 42

1 Thessalonians 3:13

1 Thessalonians 4:15-17

James 5:7-8

Note:
•   As I pointed out in the introduction to this section, there is no indication in **Matthew 24** as to who will be taken and who left.
•   The call to believers is to live holy and blameless lives so that we will not fear his coming.

2   *apokalypsis* or revelation. This is the word used in the following
    verses. What else do they say?

Romans 2:5 - 8

Romans 8:19-21

1 Peter 1:6-7

1 Peter 1:13

<u>Note</u>:
- The revelation of Jesus Christ in these verses seems to be in the
  context of judgement.
- Yet there is also the revelation of hope for those whose faith has
  been in him.
- The whole of creation will be set free from the problems brought on
  it by man's sin.

3   *epiphaneia* or appearing. This is the word used in the following
    verses. What else do they say?

1 Timothy 6:14-16

2 Timothy 4:1-2

2 Timothy 4:8

Titus 2:13-14

- Once again, these verses speak of judgement.
- The emphasis is on how we should live as we await his appearing.

There are some Christians who think that the more of a mess the earth is in, the sooner the Lord Jesus will return and this means that they have no inclination to clean up that mess.

5   What will be destroyed at that coming?
Romans 16:20

1 Corinthians 15:24

1 Corinthians 15:26

1 Corinthians 15:54-56

Revelation 7:16

Revelation 20:10,14-15

Revelation 21:4

Note:
- There is no reference to earth itself being destroyed.
- What is destroyed is everything that makes the mess on earth.
- Believers in the Lord Jesus will take part in that destruction.

6 What will happen when the Lord Jesus begins his reign on earth?
Revelation 11:18

7 How is the new heaven and new earth described?
Isaiah 65:17-25

Revelation 22:1-5

Discussion Questions
1 How can there be a healing of the nations if there are no nations to heal?
2 "The Christian hope is not for redemption from the world but for redemption of the world"[10] Do you agree with this statement? Why?
3 Is there any point in trying to find out when the Lord will return? What should we rather be doing?

Notes of Part 5:
1 Young's Concordance
2 Wilkinson, David, 2002, *The Message of Creation*, Nottingham, p.253.
3 Ibid. p.261.
4 Wright, N.T., 2008, *Surprised by Hope*, London: SPCK.
5 Bookless, Dave, 2008, Planetwise, p.76.
6 Quoted by McKeown, John, 2006, *Christian Faith and the Environment* Module Manual, OTC Department of Humanities, University of Gloucestershire, Unit 14, p.118.
7 Ibid.
8 Ibid.
9 *Book of Common Prayer*, at the end of most Canticles.
10 Bauckham, R J, 1980, Article on Eschatology, The Illustrated Bible Dictionary, Leicester: IVP.

PART 6   <u>CONCLUSION</u>

There is a proverb which says "We have not inherited the world from our grandfathers, we have borrowed it from our grandchildren."

In 1994, my brother, Professor John Guillebaud, conceived the idea of burying time capsules to be opened 50 years later, apologising to our grandchildren for the state of our world which we had borrowed from them. Joined by a number of well-known environmentalists and in the presence of many schoolchildren, these eco-time capsules were buried in ceremonies in Kew Gardens, London and the University of Liverpool's Botanic Gardens at Ness on the Wirral. Others were buried in South Africa, the Seychelles, Australia and Mexico. The thinking behind this apology is described on the website in the following words: "Numberless species of animals and plants will be known by our grandchildren only through museums and video-recordings. Whatever will they think of us? In their time there will certainly be mechanisms at work to reduce the imbalances caused by the surfeit of humans, but which mechanisms? Will it be by Nature's crude weapons of famine, old and new diseases, and ever more violence within and between countries? There is still time to reverse the frightening trends. But most world leaders are still fiddling while Rome burns - and the planet chokes."[1] Fifteen years later the situation of our planet is worse.

John also likes to consider the two great commands of the Lord Jesus in Matthew 22:37-40, to love God and our neighbour as ourselves. He asks: "are we really loving God if we do not cherish and care for all his creation, the amazing diverse flora and fauna of both land and sea, - just as we would for something made by a human loved one" and secondly that love for our neighbour should include love for 'our future neighbour'. He asks "Can we do that without greatly reducing our pollution of the planet and our consumption of the resources our future neighbour will need and, furthermore, doing our bit through family planning, to ensure that there are not altogether so many future neighbours that God's world becomes uninhabitable?"[2]

If you have been convinced, as I have, by the Biblical evidence that God loves his creation and wants his people to take care of it as good stewards, what are you going to do?

Discussion Questions
1   What can you and your family do to care for the environment
    •   in your home?
    •   in your leisure time?
    •   in your work place?
2   Is there anyone to whom you can report and be accountable to, who can encourage you in your efforts?

Notes on Conclusion:
1   Guillebaud, John, 1994, www.ecotimecapsule.com History of the Time Capsule Project
2   Guillebaud, John, 2008, "Population and Poverty: Two Sides of the Same Coin", Amplified by the same author from an article in Green Christian 65, Summer Issue.

APPENDIX 1   EXAMPLES OF ENVIRONMENTAL ACTION WHICH IS TRANSFORMING COMMUNITIES

A Rocha (Kenya)

The Arabuko-Sokoke Forest is a narrow strip of coastal forest about forty kilometres long almost the only remaining forest which used to stretch for 4,000 km from Somalia to Mozambique. A Rocha (Kenya) were concerned that the acute poverty of the local people meant that they were encroaching on this forest and many threatened species of birds and animals were being even more endangered. They established a base at Watamu, just south of Malindi beach which is a popular tourist centre.

By establishing friendly relationships with local people, and working with local pastors in Bible study and conservation discussions, they were able to show that care of the environment went hand and hand with human prosperity. Training local guides who were able to show tourists the beauties of the forest, provided needed income for the community. A tree hide and spectacular walkway over the mangrove swamps proved a popular tourist attraction and the revenue raised went towards helping local school children find their fees. This meant that rather than selling firewood, cut from the diminishing forest to earn these fees, the villagers began to see the forest as an income generating business and they now join with A Rocha in caring for the forest and mangrove swamps which now are a good nursery for many fish species, which in turn provide needed protein for the villagers.

They have shown that it is not a case of either care for the environment or care for poverty stricken people but that it all holds together. God intended that care for the environment would lead to human prospertiy and A Rocha (Kenya) have shown that it works. (See Harris, Peter [founder of A Rocha,], *Kingfisher's Fire,* Chapter four).

Farming God's Way

Some 28 years ago, Brian Oldreive was a successful commercial farmer in Zimbabwe. He noticed that his yield was beginning to decline and prayed that God would show him a better way to farm. He began to question why there is so much poverty in Africa. Then he noticed that there is no plowing or deep inversion of the soil in creation. As a result, Oldreive studied and introduced zero-tillage. Then he became aware of "the beautiful blanket over the earth of fallen leaves and dying grass [and] realized that this was a very important element in God's creation. This blanket breaks the action of the raindrop, allows water to infiltrate and feeds the soil micro-organisms." Out of these observations he developed what he called "Farming God's Way" (FGW) which became a successful tool, helping subsistence farmers in many countries of Africa. A text which inspired him was **2 Corinthians 9:8** in the Amplified Bible. *"And God is able to make all grace (every favour and earthly blessing) come to you in abundance, so that you may always and in under all circumstances and whatever the need be self-sufficient (possessing enough to require no aid or support and furnished in abundance for every good work and charitable donation)."*

"Farming God's Way" emphasises producing compost, mulching growing crops and covering the soil with crop residues in the dry season (winter). Great attention is given to keeping the crops free from weeds right up to harvest time. Oldreive noticed that if God was not acknowledged, even though his principles were followed, yield declined. Spiritual input is an important part of his training. Poor rural farmers are trained in Bible study as well as farming methods and yields have been increased as much as 300% in some areas.

Gako Experimental Farm (Rwanda)

Richard and Alphonsine Munyerango returned to Rwanda from Uganda where their families had been refugees in 1994. Richard bought a small farm at Gako, Kabuga, near Kigali, which was in a run down condition.

72

As he struggled to improve it the idea developed that other farmers were also trying to make ends meet with very little help so he developed the idea of running an experimental farm which opened in 2001 and is called Gako Organic Farming Training Centre (GOFTC). He determined to use only materials which were readily available in the country and methods which could easily be taught.

As his cow herd increased, he did in fact make a large capital expenditure not readily available to others to construct a biogas digester and used the manure to produce all the biogas needed for cooking for the training courses. After passing through the biogas digester, the remaining manure is used on the fields. This is cost-effective if there are 2 cows or more on the farm but not everyone can find the capital needed to get it going. There are now substantial grants available from the Rwanda Government which can make it worthwhile.

Other methods tried and taught included a small mound garden with a hole in the centre for the kitchen waste, which produces good vegetable crops in a small space; punctured rubber tubes for irrigation; use of old tyres to grow potatoes; collection of manure from rabbits and chickens; and many other ideas.

He also grew medicinal plants and taught their use as well as herbal insecticides. GOFTC started courses for interested farmers in 2001 and by 2009 have more students than they can readily accommodate. There are now over 30,000 Rwandans who have been trained in their methods. These ideas have spread throughout the country and into Congo and Burundi and they are influencing Rwandan agricultural policy.

They now have a demonstration farm of 0.6 of a hectare, the average size of a farm in Rwanda. Here they apply the methods they teach with a vegetable garden, growing most of the needs for an average family, together with husbandry of goats and chickens.

Care of Creation Kenya (CCK)

Care of Creation Kenya (CCK) is an evangelical mission organization operating close to Nairobi which is dedicated to awakening Christians to their biblical responsibility in environmental stewardship. Starting in 2003, CCK began its work with the simple conviction that God's people should be taking good care of what God has created.

Their mission statement is: *Our mission is to pursue a God-centered response to the environmental crisis in Africa which brings glory to the Creator, advances the cause of Christ, and leads to a transformation of the people and the land that sustains them.*

This organization focuses on promoting a God-centered response to the environmental crisis through the following activities:

- Spreading a biblical vision for creation stewardship by training churches, communities, and institutions through local and national conferences and workshops.
- Developing and distributing biblically-based brochures and publications.
- Partnering with churches and other organizations working to promote environmental stewardship.
- Advancing the development of a tree-planting culture with a focus on indigenous forestry.
- Equipping farmers to protect and improve the productivity of their lands through a biblically-based approach to conservation agriculture called Farming God's Way.
- Printing books on the environment for distribution throughout Kenya.

APPENDIX 2
PRACTICAL MEASURES TO HELP THE ENVIRONMENT WITH HELPFUL WEBSITES:

Aerobic compost heaps prevent the build up of methane gas while providing good compost. See http://www.farming-gods-way.org/Resources under "compost for small scale farmers".

Mulching and other forms of soil enrichment. http://www.farming-gods-way.org/Resources under "Decomposition and God's blanket".

Crop rotation See http://www.farming-gods-way.org/Resources under "Rotations".

Compost toilets http://www.lifewater.org/programs.aspx under "Sanitation: Latrines".

Biogas installation
In 2005 Rwanda's Kigali Institute of Science and Technology (KIST) won the Ashden Award for Sustainable Energy for installing large scale biogas digesters under Kigali Prison. The sight and smell of sewage disappeared, fuel was piped to the kitchens halving the wood needed to cook for 5000 prisoners and the fertiliser was used on kitchen gardens. (www.ashdenawards.org/winners/kist05) By 2009 6 of the large prisons have had these plants installed and others are planned. There are currently plans to install biogas digesters in 500 secondary schools in Rwanda (www.changemakers.com/node/6030 and on 28th May 2009 Africa News reported that a Dutch Bank (FMO) was to provide funding to enable small scale farmers with 2 or more cows to install a small biogas digester under a Government scheme. (www.africanews.com).

Solar Energy
On 5th August 2007 Rwanda opened Africa's largest Solar power generator on a hill outside Kigali. This generator is connected to the

national grid. (www.clickafrique.com) There are also plans to use solar panels on roofs which store energy in batteries for use at need. These would be used in Health Centres, schools and administrative centres which at present are not on the grid. It is hoped that about 15,000 private homes will also use these panels and there are plans to set up solar kiosks where batteries would be charged centrally and then rented out to private homes. http://mininfra.gov.rw/index, under "solar energy".

Wind power

At present there are no windmills in Rwanda though the Government is currently trying to produce a 'wind-map' to locate the best potential sites. This could take until the end of 2010 and then there are plans for one or two pilot projects with funding from the European Union. http://mininfra.gov.rw/index, under "wind power".

Fuel efficient stoves

Rural Extension with Africa's Poor has developed a number of leaflets teaching how to make and use fireless stoves and fuel-efficient stoves (http://reap-eastafrica.org/reap/ under "Domestic Teaching Leaflets" and find the ones on:
- Efficient use of firewood
- Making a fireless cooker
- Using a fireless cooker
- The Maendeleo Jiko

Also 'Send a Cow' produce a leaflet explaining how to make a fuel-saving stove. www.sendacow.org.uk

Wind up torches (flashlights) and radios

A wide variety of wind up torches and radios are now readily available. They use no batteries and can now last longer than before.

Bicycle generators for recharging mobile phones and other things
There are several sites available e.g. www.econvergence.net;
www.pedalpowergenerator.com or www.mobileapptitude.com .

Terracing and other methods of soil conservation

When my sister visited me in 2002, she was horrified by the soil erosion
she noticed in Rwanda. She works in China where she was used to
seeing all the hills terraced. Were she to return now she would see a
different picture. The Government has been encouraging people to
terrace the hillsides. It is not unusual to see about 40-50 people out with
their hoes having been told by their local government official to put in
a few hours of community service. Initially there were grumbles, but
now people are realising that the terraces are producing more food than
before and the soil is not being washed away. As a result, fertilisers and
organic material remain on the terrace which leads to better yields and
the retention of more water on their fields. Where trees used to be cut
down causing devastation over a large area and more soil erosion, now
tree cutting is carefully controlled and more soil is retained.

Water harvesting and conservation

My sister was also concerned that very few houses had guttering, and
there were few cisterns to keep the rain water for the dry season. Once
again, things have changed. Now no public building may be built
without gutters and a large water tank. Other forms of water harvesting
are being tried, *e.g.* digging a hole which is lined with plastic sheeting
and has a roof over it to prevent evaporation. This is not as efficient as
a water barrel but it is cheaper and water is retained for use in the dry
season.

Using bicycles, feet or public transport whenever possible rather than
cars. As I have been finding out about Rwanda's environmental policies,
I have been very impressed, but here is one area where I feel they fall
short. Instead of encouraging bicycles, they have been forbidding them
use in towns. Many areas are forbidding their use on any paved roads

in an effort to prevent some of the horrendous accidents that have taken place. If only they would instead make dedicated cycle tracks and encourage the use of cycles rather than cars.

Insulating houses (to keep them warm in a cold climate and cool in a hot one)

Planting of trees. Over the last decade 1.3 million sq km of rainforest has been lost for timber and intensive farming. In September 2006, the United Nations Environment Project asked the nations to plant 1 billion trees worldwide as a means of counteracting this loss. By September 2009, the number of trees planted worldwide had exceeded 7 billion! Planting trees is a good way of mitigating the build-up of carbon dioxide thus helping reduce global warming. This is not the only benefit: trees recycle nutrients in the soil, they prevent erosion and they keep water in the atmosphere, as well as restoring lost habitats for animals and birds and preserving bio-diversity. However, care needs to be taken about where and what sort of trees are planted. In a study in 2006, Ken Caldeira of the Carnegie Institute of Washington showed that forest plantations of coniferous trees in temperate zones are in fact carbon neutral in their effect or even add to global warming. On the other hand, planting trees in tropical zones can have a big impact on carbon sequestration. However, invasive trees such as eucalyptus or pines may be destructive of the native eco-systems.

Most environmentalists advise planting only native species or exotic species that have proved to be beneficial such as the *Moringa Oleifera* or *Leucaena Leucocephala*. Other trees that can be of benefit to the community are fruit or nut bearing trees, fodder trees, trees which can be used for fuel or building materials.
See www.unep.org,   www.treeaid.org.uk   or www.careofcreationkenya.org .
Development of tree nurseries and developing greater diversity of crops and trees on the farm are both environmentally good things to do.

Christian Environmental Action in Rwanda (CEAR) is hoping to develop tree planting in schools and tree nurseries alongside their primary aim of education of schools and churches in environmental studies and producing Bible study materials, etc.

BIBLIOGRAPHY

Bauckham, Richard. 2002. *God and the Crisis of Freedom*. Edinburgh: John Knox Press.

_____. "Joining Creation's Praise of God", *Ecotheology*, 7:1, pp.45-59.

Berry, R.J, ed. 2000, *The Care of Creation*, Leicester: IVP.

Bradley, Ian, 1993, *The Celtic Way*, London: Darton, Longman & Todd.

Bookless, Dave, 2008, *Planetwise*, Nottingham, IVP.

Guillebaud, John, 2008, "Population and Poverty: Two Sides of the Same Coin", Green Christian 65, Summer Issue.

Guillebaud, Meg, 2001, *Rwanda -The Land God Forgot?*, London: Monarch.

Harris, Peter, 1993, *Under the Bright Wings*, London: Hodder & Stoughton.

_____. 2008, *Kingfisher's Fire*, Oxford: Monarch.

Hodson, Martin J. and Margot R Hodson, 2008, *Cherishing the Earth*, Oxford: Monarch.

Jones, James, 2003, *Jesus and the Earth,* London: SPCK.

Livvi-Bacci, M. 2001, *A concise History of World Populatiom*, 3rd Edn, Oxford: Blackwell.

McGrath, Alister, 1998, *Historical Theology*, Oxford: Blackwell.

McKeown, John, 2006, *Christian Faith and the Environment* Module Manual, OTC Department of Humanities, University of Gloucestershire.

Neff, David, July 2008, 'Second Coming Ecology', Christianity Today, pp. 34-37.

Prance, Ghillean, 1996, *The Earth Under Threat - A Christian Perspective*, Glasgow: Wild Goose.

Petrie, Alistair, 2000, *Releasing Heaven on Earth*, Lancaster: Sovereign World Ltd.

Russ Parker, 2001, *Healing Wounded History*, London: Darton, Longman & Todd.

von Ruhland, Catherine, 2008, *Living with the Planet*, Oxford: Lion Hudson.

Schaeffer, Francis, 1970, *Pollution and the Death of Man*, Wheaton: Crossway.

Schudel, Renée, 2004, *Changed Minds, Changed Lives*, London:The Whole Person Health Trust.

Southern, Jill, 2006, *Sex - God's Truth*, Lancaster: Sovereign World Ltd.

Spencer, Nick and Robert White, 2007, *Christianity, Climate Change and Sustainable Living*, London: SPCK.

Stott, John, 1999, *The Birds our Teachers*, Ipswich:Candle.

Valerio, Ruth, 2008, *'L' is for Lifestyle*, Gosport, IVP

Waddell, Helen & Esther de Waal, 1995, *Beasts and Saints*, London: Darton, Longman & Todd.

Wilkinson, David, 2002, *The Message of Creation*, Nottingham: IVP

White, Robert S. ed. 2009, *Creation in Crisis*, London: SPCK.

Wright, Christopher, 2006, *The mission of God : unlocking the Bible's grand narrative*, Nottingham, IVP.

Wright, N T, 2006, *New Heavens, New Earth. The Biblical Picture of Christian Hope*, 2nd Edn. Cambridge: Grove Books.
-------. 2008, *Surprised by Hope*, London: SPCK.

WEBSITES CITED
tr. Alexander, Cecil F (1823-1895), St Patrick's Breastplate
   http://en.wikisource.org .
Anglican Church of Australia
   www.anglican.org.au/Web/Website.nsf/content/
   A_Discussion_Paper_on_Population_Issues,_prepared_by_the_
   Public_Affairs_Commission_of_the_General_Synod_of_the_
   Anglican_Church_of_Australia._March_2010
Article, 2006, "Livestock impacts on the Environment",
   www.fao.org/ag/magazine .
Article, 2007, "Why Livestock Matter", International Livestock Research Institute www.ilri.org .

Asian Wetland Symposium, 9th February 2003, www.riverbasin.org .

Barakagira, Alex and Eliezer Kateyo, 2008, "Impacts of Wetland Drainage on Domestic Water Supplies and People's livelihoods in Kabale District, Uganda", http://dlcvm.dlib.indiana.edu/archive . Church of England www.cofe.anglican.org/faith/mission/missionevangelism.html .

Guillebaud, John, 1994, www.ecotimecapsule.com .

Hategekimana, Sylvere and Emmanuel Twarabamenye, "The Impact of Wetlands degradation on water resources management in Rwanda: the case of Rugezi Swamp", http://www.irst.ac.rw/IMG/pdf/Paper_for_V_International_Symposium_on_En_Hydrology1.pdf .

Lingerbay Quarry Inquiry, Statement of Rev Prof Donald Macleod, Free Church College, Edinburgh, www.alistairmcintosh.com/articles/1995_law&religion.htm .

Mentoring Projects, Uganda, www.navigators.org/us/ministries/movingmountains .

Pickering Jordan, n.d. article, "Christians and Ecology" www.studenty.org.za/resources/ .

Rhymer, David, Article, "Where does Celtic Christianity lead us?" www.peran.org.uk .

Rwanda, Population, Health and Human Well-being, www.earthtrends.wri.org .

St Cuthberts, Article, "Celtic Christian History", www.st_cuthberts.net/celhist.htm .

The Catholic Encyclopedia, Article, "St Francis of Assisi", www.newadvent.org/cathen .

World Population video http://www.populationeducation.org .

World population www.geohive.com .

World Population Data Sheet 2009 www.prb.org .

OTHER USEFUL WEBSITES

A Rocha - an international Christian conservation organization www.arocha.org

Anglican Communion Environmental Network (ACEN) encourages sustainable environmental practices www.anglicancommunion.org/ethics_technology/

Care of Creation Kenya transforming people and the land that sustains them www.careofcreationkenya.org. The following books are available through CCK:

"Christ and Creation: Our Biblical Calling to Environmental Stewardship" by Craig Sorley.

"Farming that Brings Glory to God and Hope to the Hungry: A Set of Biblical Principles to Transform the Practice of Agriculture" by Craig Sorley.

"Let's Restore Our Land: Church and Community Leaders Working Together to Restore the Land" by Dr. Dan Fountain.

Christian Aid seeking to put an end to poverty www.christianaid.org.uk

Christian Ecology Link - an inter-denominational UK Christian organisation www.christian-ecology.org.uk

Christian Rural and Environmental Studies (CRES) runs certificate and diploma courses by distance learning www.cres.org.uk

Church of England http://www.cofe.anglican.org

Eco-congregation encourages UK churches on environmental issues www.ecocongregation.org

European Christian Environmental Network (ECEN) links Christian environmental groups across Europe www.ecen.org

Evangelical Environmental Network (EEN) encourages Christians in North America to care for God's creation www.creationcare.org

Farming God's Way - training in the best use of natural resources as well as Bible study www.farminggodsway.org

John Ray Initiative (JRI) brings together theological and scientific understanding of the environment www.jri.org.uk

Jubilee Centre, a Christian social reform organisation, seeking to connect the world of the Bible with the world of contemporary Society www.jubilee-centre.org. They have combined with

Tearfund, a Christian Relief Agency, www.tearfund.org, to do five Bible Studies on *Christianity, Climate Change and Sustainable Living* www.jubilee_centre.org/uploaded/files/resource_267.pdf

Living Lightly is an A Rocha scheme encouraging people to live more simply. www.arochalivinglightly.org.uk

Operation Noah - the UK church's climate change campaign www.operationnoah.org

Optimum Population encouraging environmentally sustainable population www.optimumpopulation.org

People and Planet, a global review of issues of population, poverty, health, consumption and the environment www.peopleandplanet.net

Population and Sustainability aims to bring together organisations involved in development, environment and reproductive health www.populationandsustainability.org

www.ingramcontent.com/pod-product-compliance
Lightning Source LLC
Chambersburg PA
CBHW071018040426
42443CB00007B/831